X-TREME FACTS: CONTINENTS

NORTH AMERICA

by Marcia Abramson

Minneapolis, Minnesota

Credits:

Title Page, 23 top, Andrew Zarivny/Shutterstock; 4, eddie-hernandez.com/Shutterstock.com; 4 bottom left, stockyimages/Shutterstock; 4 bottom right, 9 top right, 12 top left, 13 bottom right, 16 bottom left, LightField Studios/Shutterstock; 5 top, kateukraine/Shutterstock; 5 bottom, Mandy Creighton/Shutterstock; 6, Murray Foubister/Creative Commons; 6 bottom left, Kues/Shutterstock; 6 bottom right, RealPeopleStudio/Shutterstock; 7 top, Les talents de So et Bast/Shutterstock; 7 top left, PEPPERSMINT/Shutterstock; 7 top right, sun ok/Shutterstock; 7 middle left, solarseven/Shutterstock; 7 middle right, Limbitech/Shutterstock; 7 bottom, Ste Everington/Shutterstock; 7 bottom left, Edgar G Biehle/Shutterstock; 7 bottom right, fizkes/Shutterstock; 8, Ioannis Ioannou/Shutterstock; 9 top, NPS Photo/Public Domain; 9 middle, Wildnerdpix/Shutterstock; 9 bottom, Juan Francisco/Creative Commons; 9 bottom left, Fab_1/Shutterstock; 10 top, Manfred Schmidt/Shutterstock; 10 middle, AridOcean/Shutterstock; 10 bottom, Wandering Introvert/Shutterstock; 11 top, David Zhang/Creative Commons; 11 top left, WESTOCK PRODUCTIONS/Shutterstock; 11 top right, Mihail Guta/Shutterstock; 11 middle left, Gordon Leggett/Creative Commons; 11 middle right, D. Gordon E. Robertson/Creative Commons; 11 bottom, illustration by Joshua Avramson; 12 top, High Contrast/Creative Commons; 12 bottom right, Nickolay Stanev/Shutterstock; 13 top, CL-Medien/Shutterstock.com; 13 middle left, Vjacheslav Vat/Shutterstock; 13 middle right, JamiesOnAMission/Shutterstock; 13 bottom, iamjorge/Shutterstock; 13 bottom left, ShotPrime Studio/Shutterstock; 14 top, Atosan/Shutterstock; 14 top right, Glass and Nature/Shutterstock; 14 bottom, Wild-lifeBrian/Shutterstock; 15 top, crbellette/Shutterstock;15 middle left, MyImages - Micha 15 middle right, Edwin Butter/Shutterstock; 15 bottom, Milan Zygmunt/Shutterstock; 15 bottom left, Anton_Ivanov/Shutterstock.com; 16 top, Nancy Pauwels/Shutterstock; 16 bottom, Puzzle studio/Shutterstock; 16 bottom middle, Nidvoray/Shutterstock; 16 bottom right, Kazanovskyi Andrii/Shutterstock; 17 top, underworld/Shutterstock; 17 top left, Martin Prochazkacz/Shutterstock; 17 top middle, Brent Barnes/Shutterstock; 17 middle right, Daniel Huebnert/Shutterstock; 17 middle right, Piotr Poznan/Shutterstock; 17 bottom, Bogdan Dyiakonovych/Shutterstock/Avesun/Shutterstock; 17 bottom top right, Stockphotoguy81/Shutterstock; 17 bottom left,T omas Kotouc/Shutterstock; 17 bottom right, Sean Steininger/Shutterstock; 18 top, Sergei Bachlakov/Shutterstock.com; 18 top left, BearFotos/Shutterstock; 18 top right, meunierd/Shutterstock.com; 18 bottom left, Helena GARCIA HUERTAS/Shutterstock.com; 18 bottom right, Kit Leong/Shutterstock.com; 19 top, Pi-Lens/Shutterstock; 19 top left, shipfactory/Shutterstock; 19 top right, karenfoleyphotography/Shutterstock.com; 19 bottom, Photo Spirit/Shutterstock; 19 bottom left, nikitich viktoriya/Shutterstock.com; 19 bottom right, Patryk Kosmider/Shutterstock.com; 20 top, Vadim_N/Shutterstock; 20 bottom, Canmenwalker/Creative Commons; 20 bottom left, Twinsterphoto/Shutterstock; 20 bottom right, maroke/Shutterstock; 21 top, Sorbis/Shutterstock.com; 21 top middle, Dee Browning/Shutterstock; 21 middle, Lesinka372/Shutterstock.com; 21 bottom, Andriy Blokhin/Shutterstock.com; 21 bottom left, XX; 21 bottom right, Prostock-studio/Shutterstock; 22 top, Aberu.Go/Shutterstock.com; 22 middle, SunCat/Creative Commons; 22 bottom, Diego Delso, delso.photo, License CC-BY-SA; 22 bottom left, Jeka/Shutterstock; 22 bottom right, Paul Michael Hughes/Shutterstock; 23 top left, gianni31 joker/Shutterstock; 23 top right, Lena_viridis/Shutterstock; 23 bottom, Solarisys/Shutterstock; 23 bottom right, Wladyslaw/Creative Commons; 24 top, The Image Party/Shutterstock.com; 24 bottom, Followtheflow/Shutterstock; 24 bottom left, Prostock-studio/Shutterstock; 24 bottom middle, Philip Kinsey/Shutterstock; 24 bottom right, Creative Images/Shutterstock; 25 top, Chrispictures/Shutterstock; 25 top left, Viorel Sima/Shutterstock; 25 middle, AS Foodstudio/Shutterstock; 25 bottom, Marcos Castillo/Shutterstock; 25 bottom right, Monkey Business Images/Shutterstock; 25 bottom lower right, George Dolgikh/Shutterstock; 26 top, Colin Dewar/Shutterstock.com; 26 bottom, Click Images/Shutterstock; 26 bottom left, MarinaKo/Shutterstock; 27 top right, Bob Hilscher/Shutterstock.com; 27 top middle, GTS Productions/Shutterstock.com; 27 top lower right, Ian Peter Morton/Shutterstock.com; 27 bottom, knyazevfoto/Shutterstock.com; 27 bottom left, Randall Reed/Shutterstock; 27 bottom middle,Vac1/Shutterstock; 28 top left, 28 bottom left, Juan Carlos Fonseca Mata/Creative Commons; 28 top right, Kozak Sergii/Shutterstock; 28 middle right, Crackerclips/Dreamstime.com 28-29, Austen Photography

Bearport Publishing Company Product Development Team
President: Jen Jenson; Director of Product Development: Spencer Brinker; Managing Editor: Allison Juda; Associate Editor: Naomi Reich; Associate Editor: Tiana Tran; Art Director: Colin O'Dea; Designer: Elena Klinkner; Designer: Kayla Eggert; Product Development Assistant: Owen Hamlin

Produced for Bearport Publishing by BlueAppleWorks Inc.
Managing Editor for BlueAppleWorks: Melissa McClellan; Art Director: T.J. Choleva; Photo Research: Jane Reid

STATEMENT ON USAGE OF GENERATIVE ARTIFICIAL INTELLIGENCE
Bearport Publishing remains committed to publishing high-quality nonfiction books. Therefore, we restrict the use of generative AI to ensure accuracy of all text and visual components pertaining to a book's subject. See BearportPublishing.com for details.

Library of Congress Cataloging-in-Publication Data

Names: Abramson, Marcia, 1949- author.
Title: North America / by Marcia Abramson.
Description: Minneapolis, Minnesota : Bearport Publishing Company, [2024] |
  Series: X-treme facts: continents | Includes bibliographical references
  and index.
Identifiers: LCCN 2023035716 (print) | LCCN 2023035717 (ebook) | ISBN
  9798889164296 (library binding) | ISBN 9798889164371 (paperback) | ISBN
  9798889164449 (ebook)
Subjects: LCSH: North America--Juvenile literature. | Continents--Juvenile
  literature.
Classification: LCC E38.5 .A27 2024 (print) | LCC E38.5 (ebook) | DDC
  970--dc23/eng/20230804
LC record available at https://lccn.loc.gov/2023035716
LC ebook record available at https://lccn.loc.gov/2023035717

Copyright © 2024 Bearport Publishing Company. All rights reserved. No part of this publication may be reproduced in whole or in part, stored in any retrieval system, or transmitted in any form or by any means, electronic, mechanical, photocopying, recording, or otherwise, without written permission from the publisher.

For more information, write to Bearport Publishing, 5357 Penn Avenue South, Minneapolis, MN 55419.

Contents

North America: Think Big ... 4
Icy Cold to Steamy Hot ... 6
Mountains Rock! ... 8
Those Are Great Lakes ... 10
So Many Things to See ... 12
Awesome Animals of North America ... 14
The Incredible Caribbean ... 16
Meet the People ... 18
Amazing Cities ... 20
Land of Landmarks ... 22
Are You Hungry? ... 24
Fun and Games ... 26

Huichol Yarn Painting ... 28
Glossary ... 30
Read More ... 31
Learn More Online ... 31
Index ... 32
About the Author ... 32

North America: Think Big

When you picture North America, it's time to think big. The **continent** may be even larger than you've ever imagined! North America is Earth's third-largest continent, stretching from Greenland above the freezing Arctic Circle to Panama along the warm Caribbean Sea. Across the land you'll find beautiful landscapes, bustling cities, lively cultures, and so much more. Let's explore this amazing continent!

> Nearly 600 million people live in North America. More than half of them are in the Untied States.

Most North Americans speak Spanish or English—or both!

> French is the official language of **Quebec in eastern Canada and Haiti in the Caribbean Sea.**

Greenland is the world's largest island. About 80 percent of it is covered by a **glacier**.

Icy Cold to Steamy Hot

North America has every kind of climate. In the far north, you'll find a freezing, treeless **tundra**. That eventually turns into lush green forests across Canada and parts of the United States. The center of the continent has flat grasslands with mild weather. In the southwest, there are scorching hot deserts through the United States and Mexico. And in the southeast, there are steamy rain forests in Central America and **tropical** beaches in the Caribbean!

North America has all five of Earth's major **biomes**: tundra, forest, desert, grassland, and ocean.

Death Valley in California is the world's hottest spot. In July 1913, the temperature hit a scorching 134 degrees Fahrenheit (57 degrees Celsius).

Scientists had to add another notch to their thermometer to mark the continent's record low of -81°F (-63°C) in Canada's Yukon.

Most of the world's tornadoes form in the United States. Part of the Midwest is even nicknamed Tornado Alley!

The strongest hurricanes occur most often in the Caribbean and the Gulf of Mexico.

Central America relies on **precipitation** from hurricanes. Without these strong storms, the area goes into **drought**.

Mountains Rock!

From the Brooks Mountains in Alaska and Canada to the Sierra Madres in Central America, there's no shortage of peaks in North America. In fact, two big mountain ranges run along opposite sides of a large part of the continent. In the west, the snow-capped Rocky Mountains extend for about 3,000 miles (4,800 km). On the other side of the continent, you'll find the Appalachian Mountains. They aren't quite as long, but the range is older—nearly a billion years old!

The west coast of the continent has **the Sierra Nevada, the Cascade, and the Alaska Mountain Ranges.**

The Appalachians are home to some of North America's most well-known ranges, including **the Blue Ridge and Great Smoky Mountains.**

The Sierra Madres tower over parts of **Guatemala, El Salvador, southwest Mexico, and Honduras.**

Mammoth Cave in the Appalachians is the longest cave system in the world. So far, more than 400 miles (640 km) have been discovered.

Mt. Denali, in the Alaska Range, is the tallest peak in North America. It rises more than 20,000 feet (6,000 m) high.

Some of the Sierra Madres are active volcanoes. **Volcán de Fuego erupted in 2018, 2020, 2021, and 2023!**

The name *Volcán de Fuego* means Volcano of Fire.

Those Are Great Lakes

North America is home to many fantastic bodies of water, but only five of them are considered great. Near the middle of the continent, Lakes Superior, Michigan, Huron, Erie, and Ontario make up the Great Lakes. They were formed thousands of years ago by a glacier that carved out holes as it moved across the land. These lakes, and their connecting channels, are the largest system of freshwater lakes in the world. They cover about 94,000 sq miles (244,000 sq km). That's pretty great!

Lake Superior has the largest surface area of any freshwater lake in the world. It holds more water than the other four Great Lakes combined.

Lake Michigan is the world's largest lake that's in only one country—the United States. The other Great Lakes border both Canada and the United States.

Lake Michigan is known for its Petoskey stones. These rocks are formed from fossilized **corals**.

Lake Ontario is the smallest of the Great Lakes, but it has thousands of islands. A few even have castles on them.

Lake Erie has as many as 2,000 shipwrecks—more than the famous **Bermuda Triangle**!

The world's largest salt mine sits nearly 1,800 ft (550 m) below Lake Huron.

An Ojibwe legend says a water monster lives in the Great Lakes! The creature is called Mishipeshu.

So Many Things to See

The fantastic lakes and marvelous mountains are just a few of the natural wonders this continent has to offer. In Wyoming, a large rock formation called Devils Tower rises nearly 870 ft (260 m) above the surrounding grasslands. The Mesoamerican Barrier Reef, the world's second-largest coral reef, stretches for nearly 600 miles (960 km) along Mexico, Belize, Guatemala, and Honduras in the Caribbean Sea. There are incredible sights all across North America.

It took millions of years for the rushing waters of the Colorado River to form the Grand Canyon.

IT'S HARD TO BELIEVE A RIVER CARVED ALL THAT!

I MIGHT BE SMALL, BUT I'M DEFINITELY MIGHTY!

Giant sequoia trees in California can grow about 300 ft (90 m), **making them some of the world's tallest trees.**

Each year, more than eight million people visit Niagara Falls. This famous waterfall borders Canada and the United States.

The lakes of Las Coloradas in Mexico get their pink color from shrimp and red **algae**.

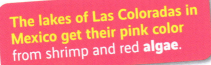

The Great Blue Hole of Belize is the largest **sinkhole** in the ocean. It's more than 400 ft (120 m) deep.

The Monteverde Cloud Forest of Costa Rica is covered in low clouds that come close to the treetops!

Awesome Animals of North America

With so many different landscapes, it's no surprise that many amazing animals are found in North America. The dry grasslands of the United States are the only places you'll spot prairie dogs. Wild axolotls live in only one lake in southern Mexico. And new animals are being discovered all the time. In 2022, a couple of high school students found two new **species** of scorpion in California!

Every winter, millions of monarch butterflies fly to a park in Mexico. Some fly from as far away as Canada.

The bald eagle is the national bird of the United States.

Armadillos come in many shapes and sizes. Some have funny names, such as the screaming hairy armadillo.

Beavers have big orange teeth that never stop growing.

Polar bears have black skin under their white fur. This helps their bodies trap heat from the sun.

The quetzal is Guatemala's national bird. The bird was so important to Maya and Aztec peoples, that only royals and warriors were allowed to wear their bright feathers.

The Incredible Caribbean

Coral reefs and about 700 islands make up the watery world of the Caribbean. But its white sands, sunny skies, and turquoise waters are only part of what makes the Caribbean so lovely! You'll find many kinds of plants and animals, including more than 1,300 species of fish, throughout these waters along the south of North America. Many people flock to the area's 13 countries and 17 territories every year. It's time for an island adventure!

St. Kitts and Nevis is the smallest country in North America. The twin-island country is about one-fifth the size of Mexico City!

The Caribbean was once full of pirates. Its many islands were perfect hideaways for ships and stolen goods.

The flying fish is both the national fish and national food of Barbados.

Cuba is the biggest island in the Caribbean. **It has the world's smallest bird—the bee hummingbird!**

People have lived on the island of Hispaniola for more than 7,000 years! **Today, it's home to the countries of Haiti and the Dominican Republic.**

Humpback whales spend winter off the coast of the Dominican Republic. Some swim as far as 4,000 miles (6,400 km) to get there.

Meet the People

People first came to North America about 20,000 years ago. As these **Indigenous** peoples spread out, the lifestyles and cultures of these groups were shaped by the different climates and conditions around them. In the Arctic, Inuit peoples on hunting trips built temporary homes called igloos from snow blocks. Farther south, the Maya relied on farming to get their food. Many Indigenous peoples keep their cultures alive today through storytelling, dance, and art.

Today, more than 450,000 people are part of the Cherokee Nation. They often gather for music and dances.

Canada alone has more than 630 different groups of First Nations peoples!

The Navajo language was used as a secret code during World War II (1939–1945). The code was never broken!

WE ARE PROUD OF OUR WAR HEROES!

The Inuit believe the northern lights show the spirits of their **ancestors**.

The Maya **civilization** built great cities and pyramids in what is present-day Mexico, Belize, and Guatemala. It's believed some Mayan cities have still yet to be discovered.

Amazing Cities

Nearly 80 percent of North Americans live in cities, and it's easy to see why! These places are full of modern buildings, museums, parks, and so much more. New York City has more than 250 towering skyscrapers and is visited by millions of people every year. Although it's popular, New York is not North America's biggest city. That honor belongs to Mexico City, which is bursting with about 21 million people. There's lots to explore!

Greenland's capital, Nuuk, is the northernmost capital city in the world!

Present-day Mexico City has been the capital of two nations! Before it became a modern capital, the land was the site of the Aztec capital, Tenochtitlán.

WHAT'S WRONG?

WE'VE BEEN UNDERGROUND FOR SO LONG. I MISS THE SUNSHINE!

Toronto, Canada, is home to the world's largest underground shopping mall. It has about 1,200 stores.

Chicago, Illinois, has been nicknamed the Windy City. It gets strong breezes off Lake Michigan.

In the streets of Havana, Cuba, you'll find history at every turn—**from old, colorful buildings to vintage cars!**

The first Panama City was destroyed by pirates in 1671. You can still see its ruins today.

New Orleans, Louisiana, is often considered to be the most haunted city in the United States. It's also famous for its food and festivals.

Land of Landmarks

Along with beautiful cities, North America is also covered in incredible landmarks. Some, such as New York City's Empire State Building, are used every day. Inside you'll find offices, restaurants, and even art galleries. Other landmarks are a part of history. You'll find totem poles of the Haida people on an island off the coast of Canada's British Columbia. The Haida people carved these structures to share their history.

The Angel of Independence statue in Mexico City **celebrates Mexico's freedom from Spain.**

The world's first underwater sculpture park is off Grenada Island in the Caribbean. Many of the sculptures are covered in colorful corals.

THIS PYRAMID DOESN'T LOOK THAT BIG.

MOST OF IT IS COVERED BY DIRT. IT GOES ALL THE WAY TO THE TOP OF THAT HILL.

Mexico's Great Pyramid of Cholula is the world's largest pyramid.

GOLDEN GATE THIS, GOLDEN GATE THAT.... WHERE IS THE ACTUAL GATE?

I'M TRYING TO FIND IT!

San Francisco's Golden Gate Bridge is named after the Golden Gate **strait** beneath it.

Toronto's CN Tower is North America's tallest structure. It's a little more than 1,800 ft (550 m) tall.

It took 10 years to build the Panama Canal. The narrow waterway creates a shortcut between the Atlantic and the Pacific Oceans.

Are You Hungry?

Next time you snack on popcorn, potato chips, or guacamole, you can thank North America! All over the continent, people turn local crops into delicious foods. Ingredients, such as corn, potatoes, and avocados, have become popular around the world, but they've been grown in North America for thousands of years. Today, these foods are used to make hundreds of mouth-watering dishes, such as corn dogs, avocado ice cream, and potato salad. What other tasty foods are from North America?

The southern United States is famous for its barbecue. Delicious barbecued meats are smoked for hours before they are ready to eat.

Machetes are a popular dish in Mexico. The giant tortillas can be 2 ft (61 cm) long and are filled with meat, cheese, and vegetables.

The humble hamburger (with or without cheese) is the most popular meal in the United States.

NO WAY! NOTHING BEATS A GOOD BURGER!

TRY SOME OF MY POUTINE. YOU MIGHT LIKE IT.

Poutine, a delicious dish of french fries topped with melted cheese curds and gravy, was created in Canada.

In Jamaica, jerk chicken is a popular dish. The meat is seasoned with different spices and then slowly smoked.

Pupusas come from El Salvador. These fluffy corn pancakes are stuffed with cheese, beans, meat, or veggies—whatever you like!

It's thought that tacos as we know them today were invented by Mexican miners in the 18th century.

Fun and Games

Want to have some fun? Head to New York City on New Year's Eve to see a giant ball drop at the stroke of midnight! Or maybe you'd rather gather with different groups across the continent to watch some sports. You might see a hockey game in Canada, a football game in the United States, or a soccer match in Mexico. There are so many ways to pass your days across North America!

Baseball is the most popular sport in Cuba. Many people play it in the streets.

In Canada, kids as young as two learn to play ice hockey!

If you're near Ottawa, Canada, check out Winterlude. People gather together to enjoy some fun in the cold.

Mardi Gras in New Orleans is one of North America's biggest street parties. There are more than 70 parades.

Belize's Carnival shows off the area's many cultures through vibrant costumes and dance performances.

Many people in Mexico celebrate Day of the Dead on November 1 and 2. The holiday is for remembering ancestors.

Huichol Yarn Painting
Craft Project

The Huichol people high up in the Sierra Madre mountains of Mexico keep their culture alive through colorful yarn paintings. They use this art, which is made by pressing yarn into melted beeswax, to share stories. Why not create your own yarn painting to tell a story?

Until modern times, the Huichol people didn't have a system of writing. They used art instead.

What You Will Need
- A piece of cardstock
- A pencil
- Colorful yarn
- Scissors
- Glue

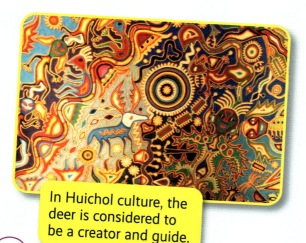

In Huichol culture, the deer is considered to be a creator and guide.

Step One

Draw a picture on the piece of paper. Keep the design simple. A sun or flower work well with this technique.

Step Two

Cut some pieces of yarn. Apply glue to a few lines of your drawing. Lay strips of yarn into the glue. Gently press down on the yarn so it sticks to the paper.

Step Three

As you fill in your picture, try laying the yarn in different shapes. Leave some areas outlined while filling in others.

Step Four

Keep gluing yarn to the paper until your yarn painting is complete!

algae tiny plantlike living things that live and grow in water

ancestors family members who lived long ago

Bermuda Triangle a part of the Atlantic Ocean where ships and planes are said to vanish

biomes areas where certain kinds of land, climate, and living creatures form natural communities

civilization a large group of people who share the same history and way of life

continent one of Earth's seven large landmasses

corals groups of rocklike structures made from the skeletons of sea animals

drought a long period of time with very little or no rain

glacier a large mass of ice formed in cold regions from firmly packed snow

Indigenous describing the people that originally lived and may continue to live in a certain place

precipitation water that falls to the ground in the form of rain, snow, sleet, or hail

sinkhole a very deep, hollow place in the ground

species groups that living things are divided into according to similar characteristics

strait a narrow waterway between two pieces of land

territories areas of land that are controlled by countries that are far away

tropical related to parts of the world near the equator where the weather is very warm

tundra cold, treeless land where the ground is frozen just below the surface

Read More

Banting, Erinn. *North America (Exploring Continents).* New York: Lightbox Learning Inc., 2023.

Finan, Catherine C. *The Maya Civilization (X-treme Facts: Ancient History).* Minneapolis: Bearport Publishing Company, 2022.

Vonder Brink, Tracy. *North America (Seven Continents of the World).* New York: Crabtree Publishing Company, 2023.

Learn More Online

1. Go to **www.factsurfer.com** or scan the QR code below.

2. Enter **"X-treme North America"** into the search box.

3. Click on the cover of this book to see a list of websites.

Index

Appalachian Mountains 8–9

Aztec 15, 20

Canada 4–8, 10, 13–14, 18, 20, 22, 24, 26–27

Caribbean 4, 6–7, 12, 16–17, 22

Central America 6–8

Cherokee Nation 18

desert 6

festivals 21, 26–27

food 17–18, 21, 24

glacier 5, 10

Grand Canyon 12

Great Blue Hole 13

Great Lakes 10–11

Greenland 4–5, 20

Huichol people 28

Inuit 18–19

languages 4, 18

Maya 15, 18–19

Mexico 5–8, 12–14, 16, 19–20, 22, 24–28

Mishipeshu 11

Navajo 18

Niagara Falls 13

Panama 4–5, 21, 23

pirates 16, 20

Rocky Mountains 8

Sierra Madres 8–9

Sierra Nevada Mountains 8, 12, 28

United States 4–7, 10, 13–14, 21, 24, 26

About the Author

Marcia Abramson is a North American who lives and works in Michigan—right in the mitten.